How To Start A Digital Marketing Agency

By: Carmine Mastropierro

Table of Contents

Introduction

Welcome to my digital marketing agency guide and thank you dearly for purchasing it. By the end of this guide, you will have a fully functioning website that your clients can use to contact you, view your portfolio, and read valuable content. You will grasp the tactics and know-how on attracting and reaching out to clients. Social media marketing, email marketing, and SEO will be second nature. You will understand the right mindsets to have getting into business that will put you ahead of many entrepreneurs. Take your time, enjoy the process, and best of luck!

Chapter 1: Mindsets

Being an entrepreneur requires you to have certain paradigms and mindsets to succeed. If you can adopt the right ideas before you start, you will greatly increase your chances of success in the end run. These are some that we believe will help you and have aided previous students.

1. **Discipline**: You need to be able to do the work consistently and for long hours at certain points. Developing discipline not only improves your business performance but overall life. You only gain it by continually doing tasks even when you do not feel like it.

2. **Patience**: Rome wasn't built in a day and neither will your market agency but with time it will be a prosperous asset to you. Remember that it doesn't matter how slowly you go as long you don't stop. The continual effort over time that you put into a business compounds and turns into something special. Be patient while building your agency, learning new skills, and during any processes.

3. **Positivity**: Entrepreneurship is exciting and rewarding but can be stressful if you make it. Always do your best to look at everything with a positive perspective. It's not win or lose, it's win or learn. See every experience as a way to improve and grow. Get excited for the work you do thinking about how much money you will make and how great of an asset your business will be one day.

4. **Don't be a perfectionist**: Perfectionism will only slow you down in business. Yes you should have that Steve Jobs drive to only deliver the best but you need to also launch products quickly. In the case of your digital agency, don't get too caught up in the little details. You want to get your website up, content on it, pages made, plugins installed and have it usable for other people. Optimisation, extra features, and small details can be implemented afterwards. It's best to get the main product out and accessible as quickly as possible.

5. **Be a risk taker**: If you look up the definition of an entrepreneur, it's usually defined as an individual who takes upon the risk of a business. Business is inherently a risk since it is not guaranteed to succeed and make you money. During your entrepreneurial journey, you may have opportunities to land big clients, iterate new features, outsource, automate and alike. These can cost money and time but can yield a very healthy ROI. Never be afraid to take an intelligent risk in business because it can greatly pay off.

6. **Make sacrifices**: How bad do you want? Do you want to make 5 figures? 6 figures? 7 figures? Are you interested in working for yourself full time and travelling the world? If so you will have to make sacrifices. This means playing video games less, watching television less, going to bed earlier, waking up earlier, and changing your routine. As the old saying goes, no pain, no gain. Consider what you could be weaving out of your life to give you more time to work on your business or to do more productive activities.

7. **Always be learning**: An entrepreneur that doesn't learn, doesn't earn. Consistently growing your knowledge around subjects like marketing, accounting, copy writing and similar will result in direct business growth. You will learn new marketing strategies, ways to get clients, and tactics for driving traffic for example. No matter what you are learning, always assure that you actually apply it and don't just forget it the next day.

If you can begin to internalise these and practice them you already on the proper path in entrepreneurship.

Chapter 2: Research & Planning

One of the first decisions that needs to be made for your digital agency are the services provided. This will of course be based on the skill sets you currently have. Ask yourself the following questions:

- What skills do I have that could help people? (Web design, social media marketing, writing, graphics design, investing, and strategic planning are some examples).
- What areas of expertise do I have that I could leverage for consulting?

Brainstorm and write all of these down. The next step is to then identify all of the needed components for these services. For example web design/development may be something along the lines of:

- Requires hosting.
- Requires a domain name.
- May require a CMS like WordPress if client prefers.
- Client may want e-commerce integration.
- A list of needed plugins or apps.
- Social media integration.
- Content or pages the client may want.

This exercise will allow you to understand from beginning to end what you need to do for each service to streamline it. Eventually you will have laid out steps from experience on how to exactly conduct various projects. It will also give you a detailed check-list to show to clients if need be.

Competitive Analysis

What better way to learn how to create a digital agency than to break down what other ones are doing? Lets take a quick visit to Google and search for queries along the lines of "digital agency" and "digital marketing agency". We suggest taking the time to perform recognizance on these businesses to take notes. Lets take a look at the example on the next page.

This is a digital marketing agency out of Toronto, Ontario. From first glance we can see they boast a simple, modern, and sleek design. The logo contrasts nicely with a blue background colour that is both friendly and professional. They also have a catchy slogan in a nice flat font. Their navigation is spaced out, isn't crowded, and also contrasts to make it easy to see.

When analysing your competitions websites, take notes of all of these little things. They know more than anyone the importance of fine details. It's not overwhelming and users can easily navigate to where they want to without getting distracted. This helps flow them through the sales funnel.

Who We Are

We are the united front in helping to end. 30 We have a job more than a digital agency - we are trusted friends and consultants. We build results oriented digital strategies and consistently refine your campaigns for optimal outcome. From full scale digital marketing and advertising strategy and planning right through to the tactical execution and reporting we've got your execution full. It's all about endorsing your brand's persona and our top creative minds make it happen with a bespoke digital agency approach. We have prime watchffices in New York, for digital and hardware, and we don't stay in between and beyond.

Scrolling down, the next thing we see is a section detailing the companies background. This is crucial so that users understand who you are, your mission, and how you can help them. They use an easy-to-read font with a related picture of their workplace right beside it. As I will touch on a bit later when creating your website, it's critical that you talk more about your customer than yourself. Sure, let them know where you are head-quartered and similar information but really hone in on how it will benefit them to work with you.

What We Do

We get results. We pore over information, big data and creativity to help make brands more profitable, shareable, and believable. From day one our goal as a digital agency has always been to seek a great return on your investment. This is win the buzzer - we've achieved for our clients making a hit has never looked better. View Recent Work.

Paid Media Optimization

Learn More

Last but not least we see a list of all of their services. This will give users an instant understanding if this agency meets their needs and they use a "Learn More" call to action. You should be using call to action statements as much as you can within your copy writing when it makes sense. This can be anything from "Schedule a call", "Email us" or anything that entices the reader to do something.

Visit a few websites and give them a breakdown detailing:

- Navigation/Header/Footer.
- Design/Colours/Logo.
- Pages.
- Content.
- Copy writing/Calls to action.
- Services provided.
- Prices.

This information can then be used to help your business attain great results by improving these areas. Don't just follow our list down to a science, jot down any ideas that come to mind while researching competition.

Creating A Lean Business Plan

With some fresh ideas under your belt, you can now take the time to create a lean business plan. In today's business world it is all about speed and bootstrapping. No longer are the days of business plans that take weeks or months to compile or businesses that take even longer to launch. Use pen and paper, Microsoft Word, OneNote, Google Drive or whatever tools you have available to you. Write down the following areas:

1. What is the product offered and what problem does it solve?
2. What demographic would be purchasing this product?
3. What is our unique value proposition?
4. What is the solution to the problem?
5. What sales channels can we use?
6. How will revenue be generated?
7. What is our cost structure?
8. What are key metrics to look for?
9. What is our unfair advantage?

Lets go over all of these in detail now.

Product offered/Problem

This of course begins by laying out what services you will be offering to clients. Is it web design? consulting? You should have brainstormed a bit earlier and can fill this out. Now the next question is, what problem does it solve? Consider why your customer would come to you and pay a fee to have you perform a service. Perhaps it is because:

- They do not have the knowledge themselves.
- Lack technical expertise.
- They want a website but don't know how to build one.
- The client needs advice on how to go about doing something.
- It saves them time, money, and energy.

When you've identified this you can then implement into your copy writing as well, an example being "Need a website but don't know how to build one? We'll do it for you". This is a very basic example but I know you'll get the point.

Demographic

Unless you have access to expensive market reports you probably won't be able to 100% identify this just yet. As you begin collecting data through Google Analytics later and get your first clients, you will slowly be able to solidify whom your ideal client is. Right now we recommend that you take the time to create a consumer profile consisting of what you believe your target demographic is, such as:

- Their age.
- Their location.
- Why they need your services.
- Education level.

This isn't overly important just yet so don't get caught up on it. I'd also recommend looking into free market/industry reports at this time. Visit Google and search for

- Your city/province/state + "market report"

- Your city/province/state + "business stats"

You should be able to find some useful information doing this. If you happen to be a student, I know IBISWorld will grant you access for free at least at the time of this book so look into that too.

UVP

Your unique value proposition is a short statement that depicts why you are better and different as a business. This is something that will not only serve as a basis for how your business operates but also can be used as a slogan or tag line. Maybe your value proposition is that you offer a free consulting session, have respectable credentials, or have special rates. There is no cookie cutter approach to formulating a UVP so take the time to elaborate what is going to make your agency stand out.

Problem Solution

Lets presume that your customers problem is that they require a website but don't know how to get one. The solution that you provide is to simply make one for them. This also boils down further to domain names, hosting, content systems, professional emails, and other related components. Brainstorm all of the problems a client could be facing and how you will solve it for them.

Sales Channels

Our website will be one of the main sales channels we utilise to generate paying clients. You will be learning several other strategies and platforms like email, ads, outreach, and more later on.

Brainstorm online or off-line modes that you could take advantage of to get your marketing agency in front of people.

Revenue

Revenue generated by a digital agency is always just in the client work but the recurring after sales. For example you may build someone a website but they pay you a monthly fee to manage it, their hosting, and social media accounts. In that case you received a lump sum for the website but now get a trickle of income from an easy monthly service that can be automated.

Write down all of the streams of income your marketing agency can generate with your services. This could be as small as charging for a domain name or developing an entire mobile phone application.

Cost Structure

Your cost structure will be in regards of two different things, your business and the service provided. Building your professional website and getting a domain can cost as little as $15 which Mastro Digital will be covering in the next unit. You also invested into this course which you could add. Besides that you won't be spending much more money on your agency unless you invest into paid plugins, themes, services, or ads later on. Next you want to breakdown the costs you'll have to invest into completing services.

Key Metrics

Key metrics are performance indicators we can utilize to know how well our business is operating. In a service business like your agency, you should be paying attention to:

- How many individuals reach out to you for services/quotes/questions.
- How many of them convert to paying clients.
- How much your social media following is growing.
- How much your email list is growing.
- Revenue and profit.
- Website traffic.

Unfair Advantage

Lastly you need to decide what you can offer that can't be copied or really sets you ahead of competition. This is where selflessness can really take a role because giving your clients that extra bit of service can make all the difference. Your agency may give free follow up advice, a free list of marketing strategies, a website operating manual or a list of good stocks to trade. It completely depends on exactly what you do for the client but think of how you could help them and at the same time stand out from the crowd.

Chapter Exercises

1. **Brainstorm your skills and how you could offer them as a service.**

2. **Fill out your lean business plan.**

3. **Analyse other agencies to learn how they market themselves and take notes.**

Chapter 3: Bootstrapping A Website

A domain name is the URL of your website that users will type in their address bar to visit it. Examples of domains include:

- Google.com
- Youtube.com
- Wikipedia.co.uk
- Yahoo.ca

They can include any alphanumerical combination and end with a top level domain(com, ca, co.uk, etc). Domain names will cost you approximately $10 for an entire year, and yes you read that right. It is extremely inexpensive to get a website up and running in today's world. One of the most reliable domain registrars that we would recommend is Namecheap.com.They offer incredible customer service, pricing, and security. Visit their website and sign up for a free account.

You should also keep them in mind if you need to purchase a domain for your clients in the future.

Brainstorm domain names that you would like and search to see if they are available. You can go about selecting a domain name in two ways:

- Create a brand name.
- Use a niche specific name.

Brand names are ones like Pierroshoes.com, Microsoft.com, or Mastrodigital.com. They are unique and have their own name while niche specific domains might be Bestwebdesign.com, Timemanagementsoftware.com, or Topcomputerreviews.com. One utilises a branding aspect while the other explicitly tells users what to expect from the website. As a digital agency, it is always best to choose a unique name to form a real brand image.

After you search for a domain name, Namecheap will display what is available and how much it costs for a yearly registration. You always want to got for a ".com" extension since it is the most well known and trusted. Add it to your cart and and confirm your order. You can then log into your account to manage the domain.

Now on the otherhand you do have another choice. You are going to get website hosting next and most if not all hosting services will offer a domain name. This makes it a lot easier since you won't have to connect the two as it will be done on your behalf. If you'd like to do this instead, skip purchasing a domain name with Namecheap and move onto the following step.

To have your website up on the web for others to visit you need a hosting service. These lovely companies host your website on their servers for a small fee. Just like your domain name, this will only be a small and worthwhile investment but is typically billed monthly. For this course, we are going to be using one of the most reputable hosts which is HostGator. Visit Hostgator.com and select "Web hosting" on the main navigation. These are affordable and powerful packages that they offer.

Choose the Hatchling plan to begin as you can always upgrade easily in the future if you wish. Sign up and complete the process to begin. On the very top of the sign up form, select that you already have a domain and enter it. This will attach it as your main domain and make it easier to get it connected.

Once you have completed the signup process, you will be emailed a link to your control panel with a username and password to login with. The control panel has an incredible amount of tools and features as you will see once you enter it. The "Popular links" section is where most of your attention will be.

Along with the email you received earlier will be nameservers that you will use to point towards your domain. Your nameservers are also displayed under the "General Information" section on the right sidebar. Lets revisit our Namecheap account to get this propagated. In your dashboard, select "Manage" beside your domain name.

Scroll down and you will see a Nameservers section. Replace the existing one by pasting in the two Hostgator servers like below. For the two to connect typically takes a few hours but it can be instant in some circumstances. Be patient if your website doesn't propagate quickly once you have Wordpress installed as it will eventually work.

Scroll down and you will see a Nameservers section. Replace the existing one by pasting in the two Hostgator servers like below. For the two to connect typically takes a few hours but it can be instant in some circumstances. Be patient if your website doesn't propagate quickly once you have Wordpress installed as it will eventually work.

Wordpress is a content management system that enables you to create content, products, forms, memberships, and endless features. With Hostgator and most modern hosting services, you can get a WordPress website up in minutes. To install Wordpress, begin by selecting the "Build a New WordPress Site" in the popular links section you were just introduced to.

It will then display a drop down menu, where you should have the domain you entered while registering available. Select it and then click "Next". You will be prompted to enter a blog name, administrator user name, first name, last name, and email address.

The blog name can be similar to your domain. For example if it's tennismensshoes.com, your blog could be called Tennis Men's Shoes. Choose an adiministrator username that is easy to remember and a password will be generated for you. You can change it if you like or keep it.

After filling out that information, agree to the terms of service and begin installation.

This will only take a short moment and you will be given a temporary password to access your Wordpress dashboard at www.example.com/wp-admin. If you are given an error upon visiting this URL then your domain is still connecting to your hosting account so be patient and it will work soon. When you are able to, you will see something like below. Ours of course will look differently with our specific plugins, settings and alike. Don't worry, we will guide you through learning all the nooks and crannies of Wordpress next.

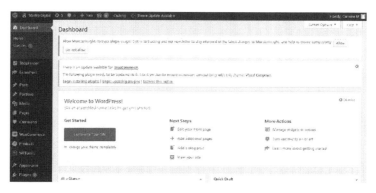

The first step to building up your WordPress website is installing a theme. Themes are rebuilt designs for your website which saves hundreds of hours that are normally put into coding. With no technical sophistication required, you will have a professional looking website in minutes. To begin lets navigate to "Themes" under the "Appearance" tab on the left sidebar.

On the following page it will display the themes you already have installed along with the option of installing new ones. Click the button below to get a new theme.

You can either directly upload a Zip file of a theme or search through their library. Click through featured, popular, and latest to see what are available.

When you select one it will bring you to a preview of the theme. Go through multiple themes until you find one that pleases you and install it. Once it is installed you can customise it by selecting "Customise" under the same "Appearance" tab as before. You will settings on the side similar to below as it differs from theme to theme.

Here are some things you need to know:

1. Simple colour schemes like black text on white backgrounds work the best for practically any niche.
2. If you can design a logo(even a simple one) then upload it in the "Site Identity" section.
3. Include useful widgets in the sidebar or footer like pages, recent posts, etc.
4. Under "Menu" select the main menu and include other pages you create after to create a rich navigation.
5. Some themes will include social media links so connect your accounts once you've created them.

Take some time to customise your theme before moving onto the next step which is installing plugins to your WordPress website.

Plugins

Plugins give your website extra functions and abilities that they normally wouldn't. This is what makes Wordpress so incredible for developing online businesses. You are able to implement practically any idea you have with plugins that are already made to do the job for you. On your Wordpress dashboard, hover over "Plugins" then select "Add new".

You can search for specific plugins on the following page or browse through featured and popular ones. To install a plugin you simply click the install button and activate it afterwards.

Here are the plugins we recommend you get:

Yoast SEO will guide you through optimising your website for search engines which is a large component of how you will drive traffic. Features include:

- Page analysis to help you improve problem areas.
- Creates XML site maps which helps Google and search engines crawl your website more easily..
- Integrates social media networks to drive traffic.
- Easily edit meta descriptions.
- Set meta tags and titles.

Security is a big concern for websites especially when it becomes a source of income. **Wordfence Security** will give you the peace of mind you need about securing your Wordpress site. Features include:

- Web Application Firewall that stops you from getting hacked by identifying malicious traffic and blocking attackers before they can access your website.

- Rate, limit, or block WordPress security threats like aggressive crawlers, scrapers and bots doing security scans for vulnerabilities in your site.
- Enforce strong passwords among your administrators, publishers and users.
- Scans core files, themes and plugins against WordPress.org repository versions to check their integrity.

MailChimp will be your go-to plugin for email marketing. It is free and very easy to integrate with WordPress. It will enable you to create email lists, send newsletters, and organise your subscribers. You can also create sign up forms and the plugin integrates with many others.

BackupGuard is one of the best tools to keep your website backed up in case of any issues. It is wise to have a backup on your computer or an external HD for a peace of mind. If you ever need to re-upload your WordPress website you'll be able to do it with ease

You will be learning how to use data collected by Google Analytics to optimise your website, its traffic, and more. **Google Analytics for Wordpress** will help you easily connect your Google account with your WordPress website to instantly start collecting useful business information.

It's simple as copying and pasting a generated code into the plugin from your Analytics account when you sign up later. Google Analytics will show you everything from where you traffic comes from, how long they spend on your website, and what content gets the most attention. This is critical information to determine what areas of your website are performing and the best and worst.

Creating Posts

Creating great content on a regular basis will aid you in ranking highly in search engines, generating traffic and converting sales. In the future to create an article, click on the "Posts" tab, select "Add new".

Use a keyword in your title and make it enticing for someone to click. An example could be "Best Strategies For Getting Clients And Closing Deals". In the SEO section later you will learn how to perform keyword research so this is mostly for later purposes.

After you have written your post, create a category to organise it on the right sidebar. Consider all of the topics you could be writing about in your niche and make a category for each one. This is convenient for both you and your audience to navigate articles easier.

At the top of the posts page you can see how many posts in total you have in your website. You can also views which are are scheduled, stickied, pending or in draft mode. If you'd like to chip away at an article over time, you can save your posts as a draft so you're able to continually work on them until they're finished. Hover over an existing post and you will see:

1) **Edit**: Allows you to edit the post.

2) **Quick edit**: Change attributes of the post quickly.

3) **Trash**: Send the post to the trash to delete it.

4) **View**: Visit the actual post in your browser to see how your audience would view it.

Tags just below this are also very important as these will connect what users search and what they find. Use tags that you believe people would use to find your article.

The featured image is a preview to your article and should relate to the inner content. We suggest using websites like Pixabay.com that have images that you can use here.

With the Yoast SEO plugin you will be able to edit the "snippet" which is really the title and description. Implementing keywords here will help boost rankings and click-throughs. The title by default is the one you entered for the post originally but you can enter a more rich description if you wish. Yoast will also give you a readability score which you can use as a basis of improving your content. If you are satisfied with your article that it meets the requirements you've learned about, post it!

You'll probably want to add images into your posts or pages at some point. With WordPress you can add pictures, PDFs, videos and more to give your readers extended resources to enjoy. You can do so through the "Add Media" button which prompts you to upload the desired file.

This places it in the media library so it can be accessed in the future if needed. After uploading it though, you can insert it right in your page/post.

When you select a file you've uploaded in the media library, you will be able to edit some of its characteristics. One of the most important ones to note is the alternative text which is covered in the SEO section of this book. This is where you will want to insert a keyword so search engines like Google understand what the image is about. Titles and captions can also be edited along with the dimensions of the image.

The alignment will change how the image is displayed in the post with three options: left, center and right aligned. You can select none if you prefer that too.

Creating daily content through writing articles is necessary for every WordPress blog. It provides useful information, tutorials, and news for your audience. It's fantastic for your SEO and driving organic traffic. When you are writing about something you enjoy, it becomes a fun task to do every day. Follow these guidelines to create the best possible articles.

Length: The length of the blog posts you write is critical for SEO and for value purposes. Most individuals will find a 150 word article too short for example. 300 word count is the minimum you should aim for every time. If you have the time, create even lengthier posts.

Visuals: Articles that are purely textual are less appealing to read. By implementing photos and videos you make it a lot more entertaining and retentive.

Links: For SEO purposes you need to utilise both internal and external links. When applicable use links to your own products, pages, and other blog posts. This creates "link juice" as you have content feeding each other back links. It's also useful if you can link to a relevant product as it can lead to a sale.

External links are those that point to another website other than yours. Use these to help the audience further understand points you discuss. It can lead to graphs, studies, and similar resources.

Keywords: You do not want to exploit the use of keywords for two main reasons. To begin, it is obvious to your audience and appears spammy. Secondly it can damage your SEO and rankings as it's considered keyword "stuffing".

Getting Ideas For Content

One of the biggest obstacles to article writing is the initial topic. To get over this road bump, we've put together some websites you should check out for ideas.

Answerthepublic.com has quickly become a favourite for marketers looking to get content inspiration. Enter a keyword into the search bar and you'll receive related queries and prepositions. Craft content around one of these ideas and you instantly will have a topic to write about.

The next website we recommend is Buzzsumo.com. This is going to reveal the most popular and trending content within any given market. Type in a search term related to your business and use the results are motivation for what to write about. While to see the most we have to upgrade to Buzzsumo Pro, it's best to stick to the free version at first.

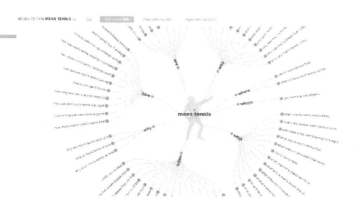

Creating Pages

Your website is going to need a few different pages to make it a complete package. On top of your homepage you'll want both a contact page and about page. To create a new one, select "Add new" under the "Pages" tab.

About Us

This page is going to tell your audience who you are, what you do, and how you will benefit them. Include the year you launched, why you built the business, and what knowledge they can expect to gain from visiting your website. Many marketers make the simple mistake of talking about themselves too much. Make sure you include legitimate reasons as to why they should be spending their valuable time reading your articles. Perhaps they are going to improve their health, feel better about themselves, get the latest news or something along the lines of that.

Contact Us

The contact page is straight forward as it serves the purpose to receive feedback and questions. You can either create a simple page that has your email on it or use a contact form plugin. Search for "contact form" in the plugin area of WordPress and there will be endless options. These allow you to customise a contact form that you can then place onto any page you like. Typically this is in the form of a short code, that you copy and paste. If you go this route, assure that the plugins settings are made to send the entries to the correct email.

Portfolio

This is where you can showcase logos, websites, and similar projects you've worked onto to future clients. Being able to see an agencies work is crucial social proof and can lead to closing deals. If you don't have any projects you've worked on from past clients, you can include mock up websites or logos to show your skill instead.

Chapter 4: Google Analytics

Data tells you everything you need to improve and continue doing in business. Without it you will lose valuable opportunities to increase conversions, website performance, and understand your target demographics. Google is too kind to us entrepreneurs with the tools and information they give us freely. Google Analytics is one of those tools and it is an absolute necessity to have it, not just a recommendation.

If you haven't signed up for an account at www.analytics.google.com already, go ahead and do so. Under the Admin panel click the Property dropdown menu and select "Create new property". You'll be prompted to enter a URL and some basic information. Once you have completed this step, you will be given a tracking code in the form of UA-XXXXXXXX-X. Copy this code and paste it into your Monster Insights plugin or simply go through the wizard it includes.

It can be overwhelming at first when you first see the various graphs, statistics, and menus. Google Analytics is a tool that will improve your business quickly and in the long run so don't fret about becoming a master soon. Over time you will understand how to measure metrics, split test, and grasp the deeper meaning of the data. You can also offer it as a service once you are experience enough.

For now lets focus on some general principles to follow that will help you build your e-commerce store. On the dashboard of Google Analytics you will first see the amount of sessions your website has been earning.

The dropdown menu on the top left allows you select various metrics and next to it you can select another to compare. Viewing your traffic levels and if they are increasing or decreasing implies if your marketing strategies are working as a whole.

On the top right of this graph you can filter by hourly, daily, weekly, or monthly levels. A monthly basis will give marketers an overall look at how their sessions or other metrics are behaving. Hourly is useful for pin pointing the exact times your website gets the most traffic, bounce rates, or similar.

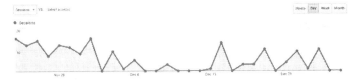

Useful Metrics to pay attention to are:

Users: Unique visitors that have had one or more sessions in a certain time frame. This is a key metric to observe as it is an accurate representation of your traffic levels.

Bounce rate: The bounce rate is the percentage of users that visit your website and leave without navigating to another page. You should analyze the bounce rates of all of your pages and content. If they tend to be higher this means that you need to adjust the pages copywriting, photos, or other content. 50% is an average bounce rate so keep that in mind when measuring your own.

Average session duration: The average duration of a users session is important to follow. If users are not staying for long periods of time this may indicate that they are not finding your website useful.

Averages pages per session: This is a similar metric to the above and is tied to bounce/exit rates. If users are not visiting more pages then it could possibly be because of poor navigation or lack of interest.

The audience tab on the left sidebar contains all of the demographic information you need to know about your potential consumers. From the country their from, the device they use, and more is available for you to analyze. This is important information as it will aid you in developing advertising campaigns and marketing strategies.

For example, click the "Geo" dropdown and select "Location". This will display the regions that your traffic is coming from. You can go even deeper into the exact states/provinces and cities. This geographical data can then be implemented when you run paid advertisements to refine results.

Under "Mobile", the overview showcases the amount of traffic that comes from mobile, desktop, and tablet devices. In 2016 and beyond, mobile traffic is quickly overshadowing personal computers thus everything needs to be optimized for phones. Too many businesses are falling behind and suffering losses because they aren't realizing this yet.

Under the "Behaviour" tab you will see what users are searching, what content is the most popular, site speed, and more. Under "Site content", pay attention to what pages such as blog posts or categories get the most positive results. If you notice pages or content with high bounce/exit rates you will need to improve them.

Google themselves have stated that a good website speed is 2 seconds or less. Anything longer than this will need to be fixed. The rate that users drop off when your website's slow is very high. This results in a loss of potential sales, sign ups, and overall conversions.

To assure your WordPress website stays quick, stay lean with minimal plugins and keep everything updated.

Chapter 5: Branding & Traffic

Social media marketing is critical for any modern business. It is a free channel to use to share content and engage your audience. Lets begin with Facebook so visit Facebook.com and create a group from the left sidebar. Fill in the information according to your business for name, location, website, etc. Include your logo and an aesthetic cover photo. I recommend you create(or get created) a graphic that has some kind of promotion. Discounts and calls to action are the best.

Make sure you input good information describing your page. Inform users what your agency can do and why it will help them. There's no harm taking the about page copy writing from your website and using it for your Facebook page but adjust some of it.

Aim for posting at least 3 times a day. Morning, afternoon, and night is a simple schedule to stick to. Over time you will be able to notice the trends of what times result in the most engagement. Canva.com is an incredibly useful tool for entrepreneurs that need to create consistent content. It enables you to create stunning graphics, documents, headers, and more.

Engaging is critical on social media so ask your audience questions. What you should ask exactly is up to your agency and what it does so here are some examples:

- What do you think of this info-graphic?
- What are your thoughts on this marketing strategy?
- How often do you use a product like this?

Creating conversations makes your brand more trustworthy and can aid your posts reaching higher in users News Feeds. This is also a wonderful opportunity to ask opinions on your own products, website design, and similar as constructive feedback.

To begin getting users to your Facebook page we have multiple options. First you should search for Facebook groups that are related to your niche. Join them or send a request to join them. Now the next thing to consider is not spamming these groups but rather offering real value. Social media networks are used for what they're named, places to socialise Engagement in conversations and post your content occasionally. You can like and comment on behalf of your page by selecting from the drop down menu on posts. Users commonly check who likes or replies to their comments and can result in them visiting your business page.

Facebook also enables you to show 10 tabs also displayed under the "Favourites" section. Photos and Likes are required tabs you will have first. Consider what your target demographic would like to see and implement it in this area.

Instagram

One of the easiest and most rewarding platforms to master is Instagram. It's an amazing hub no matter what niche you find yourself in. Create an account on Instagram.com for your business as soon as possible. Include your logo or an attractive photo along with a website link. Your bio should state what your business is about and what it'll do for the customer. If you created a discount code previously, also put this into your bio to increase conversions.

Posting on Instagram should take place 1-4 times per day. Quotes, product photos, info-graphics, and videos do very well. Remember the 80-20 rule which is 80% of your content should be value-giving and the remaining 20% can be product/service related. No one enjoys logging onto social media to have brands overwhelming them with their products. When you offer interesting content a large majority of the time, the audience is more likely to respond positively to what you sell.

Sign up for an account afterwards on Websta.me to begin performing hash tag research. You can connect your Instagram and begin searching for hash tags related to your business. Curate a large list(Maximum of 30) to use every time you create a post. What this will do is expose your content to more users which can result in more followers and traffic.

Below is a search result example for "menswear" on Websta.

What we suggest is copying this list onto your phone in a note application. Every time you go to post on Instagram, copy the hash tags and paste them under your caption. You are guaranteed to increase your follower count with this method.

If you select a specific account you will see their recent posts, account information, and analytics. Use this ability to research competitors for ideas on content and how they approach Instagram marketing. Also take note on what hash tags they use so you can utilise them yourself.

To grow your account further you should be reaching out to other brands in your niche. Propose something along the lines of:

"GOOD AFTERNOON, I CAME ACROSS YOUR ACCOUNT AND LOVE THE CONTENT YOU POST. WE HAVE A VERY SIMILAR AUDIENCE AND THINK WE COULD HELP EACH OTHER GROW. WOULD YOU BE INTERESTED IN A SHOUTOUT FOR SHOUTOUT? LET ME KNOW WHAT YOU THINK."

Most people will respond very positively to a direct message like this. From there you can send each other images from your accounts for each other to post and tag. This means their followers will be exposed to your brand and its products.

Twitter

Twitter is a great platform to build your brand and connect with your audience. It doesn't tend to fair to well for direct product advertisements. What we mean by this is that conversion rates tend to be low when funnelling Twitter traffic to affiliate links. Where it strives is when you promote articles that then lead to affiliate links.

Visit Twitter.com and sign up for an account. Upload a profile picture, cover photo, and fill out the rest of the information. Aim to post 3-5 times per day with meaningful and interesting content. Tweet at other users and join in conversations. Respond to your direct messages and be a lively brand. There's nothing worse than seeing a business that doesn't interact and looks bland.

Here is some practical advice for Twitter marketing:

- Tweet out questions to your audience.
- Make 25% of your tweets at other users.
- When Tweeting links, add your take on it.
- Never directly Tweet articles but instead add "What do you think of our latest article?", "You're going to learn a few things in our newest post", or similar.

To take time off your hands lets take advantage of Twitter's scheduling system. This is an incredible tool for automating our social media posts but it shouldn't be the end-all-be-all to your strategy. Schedule a tweet, blog post, or promotion once a day for the following week. You can then spend more time being active within the community.

It's intelligent to set some goals and understand why you're utilising the platform to begin with. It could be anything from:

1. Building brand awareness.
2. Network with bigger businesses.
3. Engage customers.
4. Drive traffic.

The next step is to create measurable milestones such as:

- Increase mentions and Retweets by 20%
- Drive 10% more traffic through Twitter by the end of the month.
- Gain a new supplier from Twitter.
- Increase follower count by 10 every day.

Pinterest

If your niche has a predominately female user base or you're in a fashion market, Pinterest is a necessary platform. 70% of the users are women thus any feminine products will gets lots of positive attention. This isn't to say you can't market to men though as there are dedicated male fashion and health lovers in abundance. The amount of male users is also increasing substantially so don't shy away from Pinterest if you have sell masculine products.

Create an account on Pinterest.com information and upload a profile picture. Pinterest works by "pinning" photos to "boards". First you have to make the boards before you can pin any content to them. From your profile select "Create board" and name it after a related topic to your business. For example it could be "Simple web design ideas" then you can then pin relevant content to this board. You want to have 5-10 boards to start with.

Search for accounts that are popular and go to their list of followers. Begin following these users every day to bring attention to your profile. You will begin to receive follow-backs, repins, and likes. This will then turn into traffic to your e-commerce store.

We want to utilise images that are long as they perform the best on Pinterest. This is the reason why info-graphics have become so popular on the platform. With a built-in analytics system, you can understand what content receives the highest engagement and at what times. Use this information to optimise what and when you post for better results.

It's key for your boards that they are include rich names and descriptions. Instead of "Web design", change it to "Responsive web design", "Lean web design", or something more detailed. This makes it easier for users searching for those terms to find your account. The descriptions should also be a in-depth idea of what people will expect from the board. "Gardening tips" won't perform as well as "Outdoor gardening tips, flower information, and garden layout inspiration" for example.

Pinterest offers a free upgrade to business accounts which includes the benefits of analytics and paid ads. Valuable information from your best performing pins to when you have the highest retention. If you have a standard account you can upgrade from your profile page in an instant. Once you have done so, you will see two new buttons appear in the navigation.

The drop down menu for Analytics displays three options:

- Overview.
- Profile.
- People you reach.

Upon selecting Overview you will be greeted by some general statistics about your account. This includes how many impressions your pins get daily, how many people view your account, and monthly statistics.

Use this information to optimise your boards the content you deliver. If you can see that a certain type of content is performing better than another, double down on it.

Email Marketing

One of the earliest forms of internet marketing is still used to this day because of its continued effectiveness and that method is email marketing. With so many platforms, software, and services available to make collecting email lists easier, you will be able to benefit from this marketing strategy very quickly. Since we are utilising WordPress as our content management system, there are many free plugins we can use to instantly kickstart our email campaigns. One of the best is Mailchimp.

Make sure you have the above plugin installed and visit the forms section. You will be able to create a new form by selecting "New Form" on the top of the page. If you don't have a Mailchimp account, it will prompt you to do a quick signup which only takes a moment.

Now there are multiple different form types you can take advantage of here. There is:

- The traditional pop up which can initiate on opening or closing of the browser.

- Embedded.

- Topbar.

- Prompts when the user scrolls.

- Sidebar.

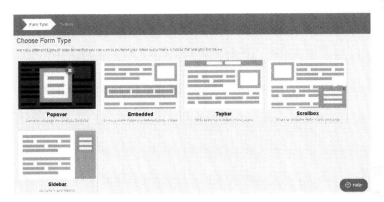

All of these have their advantage which is why we suggest experimenting with them all over time. You never know how your audience may react to one compared to another. We also recommend that you begin with the popup since it tends to have good conversion rates though.

After you select Popover, choose a theme. With the free version there are only a couple you can choose from. You will have to give it a name then customise it. Make sure to include a call to action like "Sign up now", "Sign up for the latest news and promotions", "Be the first to know", or similar. Use attractive colours like blue or orange or whichever blends the best into your website. After you've finished it you can publish it and save your changes.

You will be able to see how many people have signed up on your form from the "Forms" tab under the Mailchimp sidebar.

Creating Newsletters

Over time this number will grow and you will have a greater reach to your audience. By sending out newsletters on a regular basis you keep users aware of your brand and can potentially convert them to clients. You can send out newsletters via the dashboard on Mailchimp.com.

Create a campaign and select that you would like to create an email version.

From here you will need to follow the simple steps of naming your campaign, selecting the list you created earlier, and filling in all of the details. The email subject should be exciting and unique so take your time creating one. Mailchimp offers plenty of optimised templates for you to take advantage of as well. Depending what your goals, choose one that is relevant since they are all labelled for different uses. The newsletter should lead to your website preferably if possible. This could be to further read an article, check out new products or similar. Once you're satisfied, send it out!

SEO Strategy

If you are already familiar with the process of keyword research and search engine optimisation, use this as a refresher. For those new to it, you will learn how to perform keyword research with freely available tools to rank in search engines. You will also be utilising these keywords for paid advertising campaigns in the future. SEO is a vital component of any successful business as it benefits you in both the short and long term. There is plenty of things to learn in this chapter so take your time and re-read sections if necessary.

What Is SEO?

SEO is an abbreviation for search engine optimisation. This is the task of growing your visibility on search engines to drive organic traffic to your website. There are various aspects of SEO including back links, on-site maintenance, and more which you'll be learning about.

Many marketers make the mistake of not focusing on SEO which ultimately makes them lose out on valuable traffic. A majority of traffic is driven from search engines such as Google, Yahoo, and Bing. It only makes sense to optimize our websites to get the most out of them. If these engines are unable to find your website, pages, and posts then you miss out on potential customers, signups and alike. If you take care of your SEO then more people will be exposed to your brand and products.

It is without a doubt a complex subject but anyone can grasp the basics and apply them to reap the benefits. A small amount of knowledge about SEO can create drastic improvements to traffic and overall success.

How Do Search Engines Work?

Search engines operate by "crawling" websites and gathering data. The most relevant content in then displayed to the user depending on the search term. This is why we need to optimise our websites as then they have increased visibility.

When links point to your website from an external source, these are known as back links. They are very useful for building rank as the search engine sees your site as more important. Huge databases store all of this web information to be used for further queries. The companies that own these engines house massive data centres over the world so it can be accessed. Thousands of machines holding data process these searches every second.

The real purpose of a search engine is to provide answers for users. Any time you visit one odds are you are there to ask a question. Whether it's directions to a restaurant, show times for a movie, or looking for a job. Search engines see websites with the most traffic, back links, and fresh content as the most important. Very complex algorithms are in place to decipher ranking and there are much more variables that are considered.

So How Do I Rank?

There are practically endless strategies to ranking higher in search engines and increasing visibility. Google themselves offer advice that will definitely help improve your websites SEO.

One of the first things they recommend is to keep the user in mind when creating content and pages. This is because it can hurt your rankings when the content is different between what the search engine and a user sees. It's typically done through manipulating keywords which is known as cloaking. Having your potential customers in mind makes their experience better anyway and is a component of your branding.

The second tip from Google is top use a well structured navigation. You should be able to get from any page to another in one or two clicks through menus and links. When your website is crawled by search engines it makes it easier for it to be completed as well.

Thirdly assure that your website is full of rich content. Pages, articles, and alike should include optimized photos, internal links, external links, and good length. Internal links are done by linking to other posts or pages of your own website. External links are other websites you use as resources or to offer extra information for the audience. Regarding articles you compose, do your best to keep them at minimum 300 words long but the more the better.

How Your Audience Is Using Search Engines

Marketing stems from trying to understand how your customers feel, think, and behave. When you research this and can predict it, you're able to attract them to your products and services. This is no different when it comes to search engines. If you have a strong grasp of what they would search for, you can utilise these keywords to place yourself in front of them.

The phrases and terms used for queries are known as keywords. When evaluating the strength of a keyword, you must ask yourself the following question: If a user lands on my website after searching this phrase, will they be satisfied? Think about what they are truly after and tailor your websites content to that. Understanding keywords and researching them will be detailed later in this chapter.

Why You Need It

When you perform SEO for your business, it is not a cost but an investment. It will take time for you to rank for keywords and receive organic traffic thus it's an investment for the future. It is also one with a very high return and any successful website can agree with this. Once you have a flood of free traffic coming from search engines you'll see that is was all worth it.

One of the most beautiful parts of proper SEO is that is enhances whatever you are already doing for your business. If you have high amounts of organic traffic then you will experience an increase in sales, content sharing, brand exposure, and much more. It's a shame to miss out on something so great that you can do for free.

Where To Use Keywords

Keywords are the building blocks of the internet and search engines. Algorithms and the act of information retrieval is all based on keywords to begin with. It only makes sense to understand how to use them to their fullest potential. As websites are crawled, they are put into keyword indexes to organic them rather than keeping the 25 billion web pages out there in a single place. This allows them to retrieve information much faster and we can optimise our businesses to coincide with this.

When you enter words to search for, engines match the most relevant pages based on what we entered. The order that you type them in along with spelling and punctuation will change the results we get. One of the most important areas of a website to use keywords are in titles, text, and meta data.

Keywords that are general and short will be difficult to rank for as there will be high amounts of competition. When you use phrases that are longer and more specific, you narrow down search results and potential for ranking. These are known as "long tail keywords".

Some internet marketers exploited the algorithms used to rank for keywords and ultimately lead to them loosing their ranks or websites. In the earlier days of search engines, stuffing your content, URLs, links and alike with keywords was a viable strategy. Over time companies like Google noticed that this was happening and changed how engines decipher proper ranking.

The best practice you can do is using keywords naturally and when appropriate. Don't be implementing them into content that doesn't relate in attempts to have it appear more often on your site. The point of ranking for a keyword isn't to just be in the top search results but to actually lead the users to useful content.

Optimisation Practices

These are some effective techniques you can apply to your website to improves its SEO, rank for keywords, and make it more search engine friendly:

- Include a keyword once in the title tag and keep it close to the beginning of the tag.

- Use a keyword near the top of content, whether it's a page, article, or similar.

- In the body of your content include variations of keywords 2 or 3 times.

- To optimize both web and image search, use a keyword once for alt attributes of images.

- Use a keyword just once in a URL for pages, posts, etc.

- Put a keyword in the meta tag at least once if not more.

Title Tags

A title tag appears at the top of your internet browser and is definitely the most important area to insert keywords. It is the first place users look at in search results thus needs to be relevant to their wants or needs. The title should depict the pages content perfectly in a concise matter. This is important for both the users experience and for SEO.

When using keywords in your title tags be weary of length. If it is too long, ellipsis's will cut it off after 65-75 characters. This is plenty of space to describe your website and content to your audience so you shouldn't have much difficulty.

The most valuable keywords should be placed towards the beginning of the title tag. This helps in both ranking and likeliness of users clicking from search results. Using your brand name within title tags also helps in building brand awareness.

When a user first interacts with your website, the title tag is the first thing they'll come in contact with. It should be easily readable while also appealing to exactly what they want. When you begin to grasp these basics of SEO, you will realize it's more about creating a better user experience that ranks you higher.

Meta Tags

There are a few different meta tags but really only one you need to be concerned about and that is the meta description. This isn't used for ranking but rather to display exciting copy writing to entice visitors. When you are displayed results for a search, underneath you will see a short description for the content, this is the meta description.

When composing the meta description, do it in the same manner of your title tag. Using attractive keywords and speaking to the users needs is key to success. You will experience higher click through rates with proper copywriting in your meta descriptions. The above picture is a great example of such. You also have a bit more head-space with approximately a 160 character limit. If you do not create one of your own, the search engines will with content from your page.

URL Structuring

When deciding how you want your URLs to be structured, there are few rules you should follow. The first rule is just like the rest of your SEO copy writing and that is to make it descriptive but concise. Users shouldn't feel any confusion while reading the URL but rather be confident it will take them to where they want.

Secondly do your best to keep it as short as possible. Longer URLs are more difficult to remember, are less visible in search results, and can hinder conversions. Don't go overboard with keywords either, just one is fine enough. Use hyphens to separate words and exclude symbols or parameters that can cause confusion.

Keyword Research

With all the talk of keywords, you're probably wondering how you can actually research them. In today's world it's not about traffic, it's about getting the right traffic. Finding and ranking for the correct keywords can make or break a business. In this section you will learn how to use Google's Keyword Planner tool to analyse keywords and their respective data.

Take a visit to Adwords.google.com and sign up for a free account. Once you have completed this, you will access to many tools and analytics. Under the "Tools" drop down menu select "Keyword Planner".

On the next page select the first option "Search for new keywords using a phrase, website or category". This will expand the drop down with many options to choose from. In the first dialog box labelled "Your product or service" enter a word or phrase like "Your city" + "Digital marketing agency". Everything else can be left default but assure targeting is set to your country only and broad search is enabled under "Keyword options".

You will now thrown into the heart of the keyword planner where magic happens. In front of you will be displayed keywords, adgroup ideas, and much more. The main data we are paying attention to is the keyword, competition, search volume, and suggest big.

Now the competition level tells you how many advertisers are bidding to have their ad displayed for that keyword. It is not telling you how many people are trying to rank for it, make sure you understand that. Suggested bid is the amount you would be paying when a user clicks your ad displayed for that keyword.

Not all keywords are made equal. Remember that long tail keywords with more length to them are ideal. Other good keywords could be your city name followed by individual services.

We want to compile a list of close to 10 keywords that have a low to medium competition, at least tens of monthly searches, and has lower search results. To test a keyword that looks feasible, enter it into Google and look at how many results are given. If it is less than 1,000,000 you should keep it, otherwise there is probably too much competition.

In the long run we want to be able to rank highly for search terms revolved around services and being a digital agency in your city. As you will learn later, getting clients doesn't always involve reaching out to them but can occur when they reach out first. By generating organic traffic, you increase the chances of local users finding your business and becoming paying clientele.

Chapter 6: Getting Clients

Offline

The classic approach to physically visiting businesses and offering your services will never go out of style. Don't be nervous to do this as a new agency as it builds experience and gives you a great first impression. You will stand out much more than other freelancers and agencies that aren't doing so.

To make the best out of offline client searching you should optimally be armed with business cards. These you can get in bulk for cheap on websites like Vistaprint.com but feel free to find other services to do so if you wish. You should have this information on the card:

- Agency name.
- Website URL.
- Social media names. (Keep them the same for convenience).
- Email.
- A short statement on what you offer.

Now when you set out to go visit businesses you should be dressed professionally and groomed to create a good image for your agency. Ask to speak to a manager or someone in a higher position. If you are not able to, simply leave your business card and go on your way. If you manage to get their time for a few minutes, your pitch should be quick and could be along the lines of:

*"HI, I'M THE PRESIDENT OF **Digital Marketing Agency** AND WANTED TO SCHEDULE A PHONE CALL OR MEETING TO DISCUSS GROWING YOUR ONLINE PRESENCE. WE OFFER X services THAT WILL IMPROVE YOUR SALES, TRAFFIC, AND GET YOU MORE LEADS."*

Of course don't go off of a script like a robot and make it much more personal. If they seem interested, schedule a time to have a meeting or phone call to further discuss services, pricing, and what you could do for them.

Emailing

Cold emailing can have fantastic results and get you plenty of clients when done right. Compared to cold calling and traditional methods of outreach to clients, cold emailing has a far higher scale and magnitude that can't be compared. With email you can reach potentially hundreds of people in a day if you were seriously dedicated enough while with calling you would only reach a small percentage of that. We're not advocating you email 200-300 businesses a day, but it requires much less effort and you're able to reach many more prospects.

To begin lets go to Google and type in keywords such as:

- Your city name + "Lawyer"
- Your city name + "Dentist"
- your city name + "Plumber"

Continue with this pattern to find local businesses and visit their websites. Now not all websites will have an email but rather a phone number. You should write this phone number down or keep it in an excel sheet for later use. At the moment we are focusing on emailing prospects so search for businesses that offer an email to contact them at. When you do, you want to stand out from other service providers. The next page has some points you should follow when contact businesses that will greatly increase your chance of them responding positively.

- Not using a spam-like subject line. I have had had the best success using "Business inquiry" as it is simple, general, and tends to have much higher click rates than "SEO Service", "Consulting Offer" and similar. Many business owners don't even open those since they receive so many and instantly delete them. Experiment of course and test out various subject lines to see which gets the best results.
- Providing a mockup of what you can do if its design related. This is huge for web design and can land you clients instantly. What is going to get better results, a business that only sends a block of text or one that shows an example of how the prospects website could look like? The latter of course. Mockups can be done through HTML/CSS, WordPress, Shopify, or even Photoshop as long as you can actually recreate it.

- Speaking about benefits and not just features. Many marketers in general fail because they only cover what features and services to expect. Instead you should mention how the client will experience an increase in sales, leads, clients for themselves, traffic, etc. Many of them may not be fluent in the business-speak you use so use their language which is **results**.

Here is a sample email that you can edit yourself:

Subject: Business inquiry

Body: Good morning,

*I am the president of **Digital Marketing Agency** and recently came across your business through a local directory. I believe we could help you improve your web presence, site traffic, and leads through a revamp of your web design and social media marketing. We went ahead and took the liberty to create a mockup of what your website could look like after we've finished it and attached it to this email. I look forward to hearing from you.*

You don't want to be writing long-winded emails that bore the reader or take too much time to get to the main point. A straight to the point email stands out drastically in the sea of spam and novels some businesses receive. If you can find the name of the individual your emailing, assure to include it to make it much more personal.

Closing the Deal

If they reply then you have a wonderful opportunity to close a deal. The goal is to keep it moving forward so schedule a time you could call them via phone or Skype to further discuss arrangements. Tell them more about your agency and how you can help them. Figure out their exact needs and cross-pollinate that with your own skills to solve their problem. Some prospects may even be completely comfortable speaking only through email because they can take their own pace.

When you finally have a client that is interested in receiving the service, you will need to draft a short contract. We believe in business you should always simplify processes especially when it involves a third party because it makes it much easier. In this regard, your contract shouldn't have tons of fine print and be intimidating to read. It can be very short in some circumstances but should include:

- Agreement that you will complete **X** service in **X a**mount of time.
- That the client will pay you **X** amount for the service.
- A detailed description of what the service entails.
- How often you will update the client.
- Who owns the website after its delivered.
- Confidentiality.

Here is a template that you can use and edit to suit your services:

Between [Digital Marketing Agency]

And [Your Clients Name].

Summary:

We'll always do our best to fulfill your needs and meet your expectations, but it's important to have things written down so that we both know what's what, who should do what and when, and what will happen if something goes wrong. In this contract you won't find any complicated legal terms or long passages of unreadable text. We've no desire to trick you into signing something that you might later regret. What we do want is what's best for both parties, now and in the future.

So in short;

*You **customer name,** located at **customer address** ("You") are hiring us **Digital Marketing Agency** ("We or Us") to:*

- *__Design and develop a web site(Or whichever service)__*

*For the estimated total price of **total** as outlined in our previous correspondence.*

Of course it's a little more complicated, but we'll get to that.

What do both parties agree to?

You: You have the authority to enter into this contract on behalf of yourself, your company or your organisation. You'll give us the assets and information we tell you we need to complete the project. You'll do this when we ask and provide it in the formats we ask for. You'll review our work, provide feedback and approval in a timely manner too. Deadlines work two ways, so you'll also be bound by dates we set together. You also agree to stick to the payment schedule set out at the end of this contract.

Us: We have the experience and ability to do everything we've agreed with you and we'll do it all in a professional and timely manner. We'll endeavour to meet every deadline that's set and on top of that we'll maintain the confidentiality of everything you give us.

Design

We create look-and-feel designs, and flexible layouts that adapt to the capabilities of many devices and screen sizes. We create designs iteratively and use predominantly HTML and CSS so we won't waste time mocking up every template as a static visual. We may use visuals to indicate a creative direction (colour, texture and typography.) We call that 'atmosphere.'

You'll have plenty of opportunities to review our work and provide feedback. We'll either share a Dropbox, Google Drive folder or Github repository or development site with you and we'll have regular, possibly daily contact.

If, at any stage, you change your mind about what you want to be delivered and are not happy with the direction our work is taking you'll pay us in full for the time we've spent working with you until that point and terminate this contract.

Text content

Unless agreed separately, we're not responsible for inputting text or images into your content management system or creating every page on your website. We provide professional copywriting and editing services, so if you'd like us to create new content or input content for you, we can provide a separate estimate for that.

Graphics and photographs

You should supply graphic files in an editable, vector digital format. You should supply photographs in a high resolution digital format. If you choose to buy stock photographs, we can suggest stock libraries. If you'd like us to search for photographs for you, we can provide a separate estimate for that.

HTML, CSS and JavaScript

We deliver web page types developed from HTML markup, CSS stylesheets for styling and unobtrusive JavaScript for feature detection, poly-fills and behaviours.

Browser testing

Browser testing no longer means attempting to make a website look the same in browsers of different capabilities or on devices with different size screens. It does mean ensuring that a person's experience of a design should be appropriate to the capabilities of a browser or device.

We test our work in current versions of major desktop browsers including those made by Apple (Safari), Google (Chrome), Microsoft (Edge), Mozilla Firefox and Opera. We'll also test to ensure that people who use Microsoft Internet Explorer 11 for Windows get an appropriate experience. We won't test in other older browsers unless we agreed separately. If you need an enhanced design for an older browser, we can provide a separate estimate for that.

Mobile browser testing

Mobile browser testing Testing using popular smaller screen devices is essential in ensuring that a person's experience of a design is appropriate to the capabilities of the device they're using. We test our designs in:

iOS 9: Safari, Google Chrome Android: Google Chrome on Android Emulator

We won't test in Blackberry, Opera Mini/Mobile, specific Android devices, Windows or other mobile browsers unless we agreed separately. If you need us to test using these, we can provide a separate estimate for that.

Technical support

We're not a website hosting company so we don't offer support for website hosting, email or other services relating to hosting. You may already have professional hosting and you might even manage that hosting in-house; if you do, great. If you don't, we can set up an account for you at one of our preferred hosting providers. We can set up your site on a server, plus any statistics software such as Google Analytics and we can provide a separate estimate for that. Then, the updates to, and management of that server will be up to you.

Search engine optimisation (SEO)

We don't guarantee improvements to your website's search engine ranking, but the web pages that we develop are accessible to search engines.

Changes and revisions

We don't want to limit your ability to change your mind. The price at the beginning of this contract is based on the number of weeks that we estimate we'll need to accomplish everything you've told us you want to achieve, but we're happy to be flexible. If you want to change your mind or add anything new, that won't be a problem as we'll provide a separate estimate for those additional weeks.

Legal

We'll carry out our work in accordance with good industry practice and at the standard expected from a suitably qualified person with relevant experience.

That said, we can't guarantee that our work will be error-free and so we can't be liable to you or any third-party for damages, including lost profits, lost savings or other incidental, consequential or special damages, even if you've advised us of them.

Your liability to us will also be limited to the amount of fees payable under this contract and you won't be liable to us or any third-party for damages, including lost profits, lost savings or other incidental, consequential or special damages, even if we've advised you of them.

Finally, if any provision of this contract shall be unlawful, void, or for any reason unenforceable, then that provision shall be deemed severable from this contract and shall not affect the validity and enforceability of any remaining provisions.

Intellectual property rights

Just to be clear, "Intellectual property rights" means all patents, rights to inventions, copyright (including rights in software) and related rights, trademarks, service marks, get up and trade names, internet domain names, rights to goodwill or to sue for passing off, rights in designs, database rights, rights in confidential information (including know-how) and any other intellectual property rights, in each case whether registered or unregistered and including all applications (or rights to apply) for, and renewals or extensions of, such rights and all similar or equivalent rights or forms of protection which subsist or shall subsist now or in the future in any part of the world.

First, you guarantee that all elements of text, images or other artwork you provide are either owned by your good selves, or that you've permission to use them. When you provide text, images or other artwork to us, you agree to protect us from any claim by a third party that we're using their intellectual property.

We guarantee that all elements of the work we deliver to you are either owned by us or we've obtained permission to provide them to you. When we provide text, images or other artwork to you, we agree to protect you from any claim by a third party that you're using their intellectual property. Provided you've paid for the work and that this contract hasn't been terminated, we'll assign all intellectual property rights to you as follows:

You'll own the website we design for you plus the visual elements that we create for it. We'll give you source files and finished files and you should keep them somewhere safe as we're not required to keep a copy. You own all intellectual property rights of text, images, site specification and data you provided, unless someone else owns them.

We'll own any intellectual property rights we've developed prior to, or developed separately from this project and not paid for by you. We'll own the unique combination of these elements that constitutes a complete design and we'll license its use to you, exclusively and in perpetuity for this project only, unless we agree otherwise.

Displaying our work

We love to show off our work, so we reserve the right to display all aspects of our creative work, including sketches, work-in-progress designs and the completed project on our portfolio and in articles on websites, in magazine articles and in books.

Payment schedule

We're sure you understand how important it is as a small business that you pay the invoices that we send you promptly. As we're also sure you'll want to stay connected, you agree to stick tight to the following payment schedule.

Payment schedule

We issue invoices electronically. Our payment terms are [number] days from the date of invoice by PayPal. All proposals are quoted in [currency] and payments will be made at the equivalent conversion rate at the date the transfer is made.

You agree to pay all charges associated with international transfers of funds. The appropriate bank account details will be printed on our electronic invoice. We reserve the right to charge interest on all overdue debts at the rate of [percentage] per month or part of a month.

----

*Signed by and on behalf of **company name***

*Signed by and on behalf of **customer name***

Date

Everyone should sign above and keep a copy for record.

When you send this to your client, they can use mostly any PDF reading software to edit it and add their signature to the bottom. Once this is sent back to you and reviewed, you can issue the payment which you will learn how to in the next section. Feel free to edit this template to your liking and exact needs.

Collecting payments from your clients is quick and easy with freely available tools. If you don't already have an account with PayPal, we highly suggest that you sign up for a free account on Paypal.com

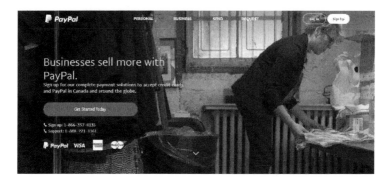

You'll be prompted to enter some basic information and then link a credit card or bank information to receive payments. PayPal acts as both a payment gateway processor and merchant account. This means they will help you transact payments and keep the money in an account that you can move around.

For our clients we will want to send a payment link through email which you can access through the "Tools" drop down menu once you've logged in.

Tools ∨   More ∨

Business Setup

Invoicing

Request Money

Resolution Centre

Send Money

All Tools

Next select the blue "Create" button which will take you to the following page where you can fill out the invoice details. Include a company logo to make it much more professional and trustworthy. The billing email should be your clients and Cc is the email you'd like it to return to.

Below here you will set the invoice amount, item name, description, and type of currency you would like to bill in.

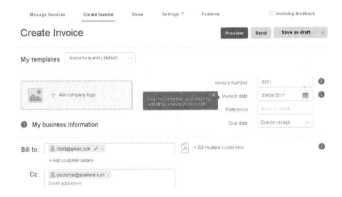

For the terms and conditions you can copy in your contract if you'd like or take the time to write a more condensed version of it. You can also attach an extra copy of the contract through the "Attach Files" on the bottom left. Once you are satisfied with the invoice and it's details, send it away!

Directories

There's no rule that states agencies have to reach out to prospects and clients. You will definitely find paying clients by them coming to you if you advertise in the right places. This is where local business directories come into play and serve as an invaluable tool. Visit Google and search for business directories in your city, town, province or country.

You will be able to find a plethora of business directories like the above example. These will typically offer the opportunity to sign up for a free account and to submit your business. Enter as much information as possible including:

- A logo.
- A detailed description of your services and benefits.
- Your location.
- A mission statement with calls to action.
- Images of your portfolio or mockups if available.
- A link to your website.
- Social media links.
- Your email.

From there your job is done once it gets submitted and approved. Locals looking for your services will stumble upon your page and reach out to you. It's your duty to turn that prospect into a client through pitching them a great service and product.

Classifieds

Similar to business directories, classified ads are a free medium to advertise your services to local prospects. Depending on where you live you may have different local ad platforms but Kijiji are a great source most can utilise.

Visit Kijiji.com and sign up for an account. Once you confirm your account, select "Post Ad" in the top right corner.

The first step is to choose which category your ad will fall under which will be services. Under services you can choose something more exact which helps users find your listing easier. Choose the basic ad option which is free and keeps the listing up for 60 days.

Your ad title should be unique and enticing while accurately describing what you can offer to people. In the description you can go in-depth on what you can do for clients and what benefits they can expect to experience. You are allowed to include a link in your description as long as it leads to further information. Adjust the location so its accurate and include any images you find will be useful for your prospects. After that simply just submit it and it will be instantly posted.

From your profile page you will be able to view how many users have visited your listing and what page it's currently on. When someone messages you it will be forwarded to your email. This is a free strategy that can easily net you many clients in the long haul.

Freelance Platforms

To grow your portfolio, earn income, and get valuable experience it's wise to utilize freelance platforms. These will allow you to make money and get your feet wet which is very valuable if you're new to client work. The first platform we'd like to cover is one of the biggest and it's called Upwork.com.

Many successful companies and agencies use these websites to generate revenue, portfolio items, and improve brand awareness. Upwork first requires you to submit an application during the signup process. If they find that there is room for your skills they will allow you to use the platform. This is to simply avoid over-saturation for certain categories like application development for example.

Upwork operates by being able to seek work that other businesses offer. You are also able to accept invitations if previous clients are interested in receiving your work again. Freelancers are able to prove their skills by taking tests that are then publicly shown on your profile. This displays your skill level to potential clients and Upwork also boasts a streamlined hiring process. It will find work that is relevant to your speciality, show others your history/reviews, and features a great messaging system. They've even created a mobile app to have better communication.

There are multiple payment options where you prefer PayPal, wire, or bank transfer. You can count on Upwork for secure and quick payments with hourly or fixed price projects.

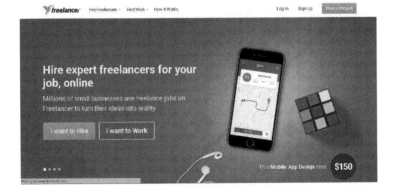

Freelancer.com is the next freelance platform you should check out. There's no harm in signing up for multiple services like this because it increases the amount of potential clients you can reach. These websites alone could result in a healthy source of income for your agency.

No matter if you offer web development, legal advice, financial services or anything inbetween, Guru is a fantastic platform to help you get your first few clients. Sign up for a free account and create a detailed profile that will give other users a good understanding of what you can do. From there you can search for relevant jobs that like the previous platforms offer an hourly or fixed price payment.

There are literally dozens of freelance platforms out there to take advantage of as a digital agency. Search for more if you'd like and use them as a way to get clients, generate revenue or even to forward to your own website.

Chapter Exercises

1. **Sign up for a freelance network, fill out your account and use to find gigs.**

2. **Create local classified ads offering your services.**

3. **Email local businesses offering your services to them.**

4. **Submit your business to a directory.**

Chapter 7: Scaling Your Agency

If you've reached this far in the course, congratulations first of all! At this point, you should have:

- A WordPress website running with your own domain name.
- Social media accounts made around your agency.
- A lean business plan filled out.

This is the foundation of your digital marketing agency and now the goal is to begin getting clients. Be patient as it can take time but once you get your first client you will remember that feeling for the rest of your life. Your routine should mostly consist of:

- Maintaining your website, optimising it, and adding content.
- Reaching out to clients via email, creating ads, social media, and the strategies you learned earlier.
- Social media marketing consistently.
- Emailing out newsletters once your subscriber list grows.
- Educating yourself on internet marketing topics.

- Reviewing Google Analytics for useful insight.
- Working on client projects.

You don't have to be doing all of these every single day as long as you gradually work on everything. Over time you will build you portfolio, grow your brand and increase your list of clients. Building a marketing agency is an exciting journey so take your time on all of the steps and I wish you the best of luck.

Printed in Great Britain
by Amazon